Introduction

It's hard to walk through a quilt store and not be charmed by the different collections that fabric companies have put together featuring their newest fabrics. There are many ways that these new collections are bundled—charm packs of 5" squares, 10" square packs and even fat quarter groupings. But the question of what to make with these collections may enter your mind. We have solved this dilemma for you. Within the pages of this book, you'll find several unique designs, ranging from table runners to throw quilts, that use 5" and 10" squares as well as two designed to use fat quarters.

Pull up a chair and grab your favorite beverage while you browse through these pages and start planning your next project. We're sure this will be a book that you'll return to time and time again for projects for your own home or a quick gift for family or friends.

Table of Contents

Inspiration

"There was a very popular mid-century door design that had three small rectangular glass panels cascading down on the upper portion of the door. Playing on that design element, New Growth spins those rectangles around a central point to create a dynamic quilt design." —Lyn Brown

New Growth

Enhanced rail fence blocks twist around a center point, creating a unique design.

Design by Lyn Brown Quilted by Cindy Cruse

Skill Level

Confident Beginner

Finished Sizes

Quilt Size: 54" x 75"
Block Size: 17" x 17"
Number of Blocks: 6

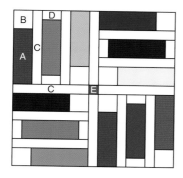

New Growth
17" x 17" Finished Block
Make 6

Materials

- 3 yards total assorted blue and green tonals or 1 pack of 10" squares*
- 3 yards white solid*
- 1 yard green tonal*
- 5 yards backing*
- 62" x 83" batting
- Thread
- Basic sewing tools and supplies

Fabric from Hoffman California-International Fabrics used to make sample.

Project Notes

Read all instructions before beginning this project.

Stitch right sides together using a ¼" seam allowance unless otherwise specified.

Materials and cutting lists assume 40" of usable fabric width for yardage.

Arrows indicate directions to press seams.

WOF – width of fabric
HST – half-square triangle ◺
QST – quarter-square triangle ⊠

Cutting

From assorted blue and green tonals cut:

- 82 (3½") J squares
- 72 (2½" x 6½") A rectangles
- 6 (1½") E squares

From white solid cut:

- 3 (6¾" x WOF) strips, stitch short ends to short ends, then subcut into:
    2 (6¾" x 49") I border strips
- 3 (6¼" x WOF) strips, stitch short ends to short ends, then subcut into:
    2 (6¼" x 56½") H border strips
- 2 (3" x 37") G rectangles
- 3 (3" x 17½") F rectangles
- 48 (2½") B squares
- 72 (1½" x 8½") C rectangles
- 48 (1½" x 2½") D rectangles

From green tonal cut:

- 7 (2½" x WOF) binding strips

Completing the Blocks

1. Sew a white B square to an assorted tonal A rectangle as shown (Figure 1). Make 48.

Make 48

Figure 1

2. Sew a white C rectangle to right edge as shown to make unit A (Figure 2). Make 48.

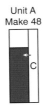

Unit A
Make 48

Figure 2

3. Sew a white D rectangle to each short end of an assorted tonal A rectangle to make unit B (Figure 3). Make 24.

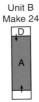

Unit B
Make 24

Figure 3

4. Sew together one A unit and one B unit as shown (Figure 4). Make 24.

Make 24

Figure 4

5. Referring to Figure 5, rotate and sew one unit A to right edge as shown to complete a new growth unit. Make 24.

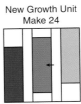

New Growth Unit
Make 24

Figure 5

6. Sew white C rectangle to right edge of a new growth unit to make unit C (Figure 6). Make 12.

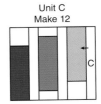

Unit C
Make 12

Figure 6

7. Referring to Figure 7, sew together one unit C and one new growth unit as shown to complete a half block. Make 12.

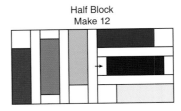

Half Block
Make 12

Figure 7

8. Sew together one assorted tonal E square and two white C rectangles to make sashing strip (Figure 8). Make six.

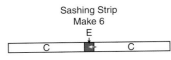

Sashing Strip
Make 6

E

C   C

Figure 8

9. Sew together two half blocks and one sashing strip to complete a New Growth block (Figure 9). Make six.

New Growth Block
Make 6

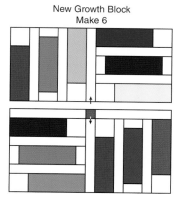

Figure 9

Completing the Quilt

1. Sew together two New Growth blocks and one white F rectangle to make a row (Figure 10). Make three.

Make 3

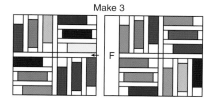

Figure 10

2. Refer to the Assembly Diagram for the following steps. Lay out the rows and white G rectangles as shown. Sew together to make quilt center.

3. Sew the H and I border strips to the quilt top in alphabetical order.

4. Sew 23 assorted tonal J squares into a row. Make two. Join to sides of quilt center.

5. Sew 18 assorted tonal J squares into a row. Make two. Join to top and bottom of quilt center.

6. Layer, baste, quilt as desired and bind referring to Quilting Basics. The photographed quilt was quilted with a floral design. ●

Here's a Tip

New Growth is made in the teal family of colors but would look great in just about any color combination. Watch orientation of units and blocks carefully when assembling.

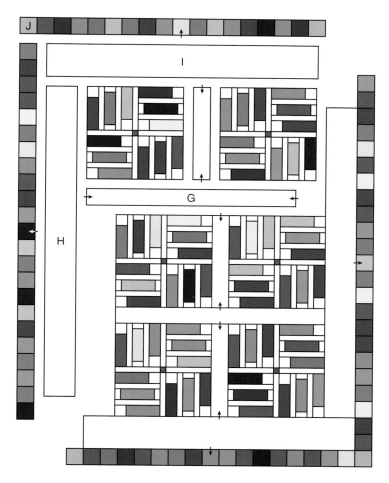

New Growth
Assembly Diagram 54" x 75"

Inspiration

"Use just twelve 10" squares to create this cheerful modern table runner. With a few diagonal seams and cuts, each pair of squares transforms into two rectangle and four quarter-square triangle units with minimal waste." —Amy Krasnansky

March of Diamonds

This table runner brings the beach into your home with bright colors and seashore-themed batiks.

Designed & Quilted by Amy Krasnansky

Skill Level
Confident Beginner

Finished Size
Runner Size: 57" x 12"

Materials
- 6 blue batik (10") precut squares
- 6 peach batik (10") precut squares
- ⅓ yard medium blue batik
- 1 yard backing
- 16" x 65" batting
- Fabric marking pen or pencil that contrasts with blue batiks
- Thread
- Basic sewing tools and supplies

Project Notes
Read all instructions before beginning this project.

Stitch right sides together using a ¼" seam allowance unless otherwise specified.

Materials and cutting lists assume 40" of usable fabric width for yardage.

Arrows indicate directions to press seams.

WOF – width of fabric
HST – half-square triangle ◻
QST – quarter-square triangle ⊠

Cutting

From medium blue batik cut:
- 4 (2½" x WOF) binding strips

Completing the Units

1. Sort the blue and peach batik squares by value (darkest blue with darkest peach, lightest blue with lightest peach, etc.). Pin the pairs together to stay organized, and work with one pair at a time.

2. Mark a horizontal line on the wrong side of a blue square (see the pink line in Figure 1). Cut the blue square in half vertically to make two rectangles (see the green line in Figure 1). Mark sewing lines on the blue rectangles as shown. Place the marked blue rectangles on a peach square side by side, right sides together, aligning raw edges.

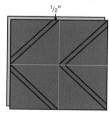

Figure 1

3. Stitch on each of the eight sewing lines (Figure 2).

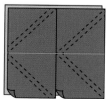

Figure 2

4. Cut on the horizontal line and midway between each pair of stitching lines (Figure 3a). Open and press. You will now have a set of four HST units and two rectangle units. Repeat steps 2–4 with all six sets of fabric squares to make a total of 24 HST units and 12 rectangle units (Figure 3b).

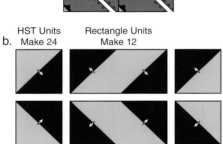

Figure 3

5. Draw a diagonal line on the wrong side of any HST unit, perpendicular to the seam line (Figure 4a). Place the marked HST unit on a matching HST unit, right sides together and blue and peach fabrics facing each other. Sew ¼" from each side of the marked line. Cut on the marked line. Open, press and trim the two QST units to 3½" square, centering the seam lines (Figure 4b). Repeat for all 12 pairs of matching HST units. You will have 24 QST units total.

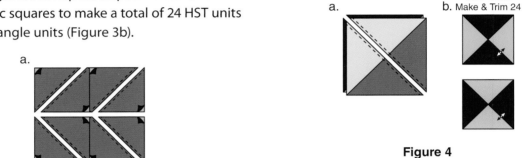

Figure 4

Completing the Runner

1. Referring to the Assembly Diagram, lay out two identical rows of six rectangle units each and one row of 19 QST units. Arrange the values as shown. You will have five QST units left over.

2. Sew the units into rows and join the rows to complete the runner. Press.

3. Layer, baste, quilt as desired and bind referring to Quilting Basics. The photographed runner was quilted with echoing diagonal lines on the rectangle rows and overlapping circles (orange peel) on the QST row. ●

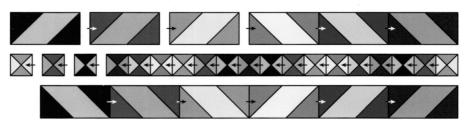

March of Diamonds
Assembly Diagram 57" x 12"

Sugar Lane

Combine two different pinwheel blocks for this sweet design.

Designed & Quilted by Jill Metzger

Skill Level
Confident Beginner

Finished Sizes
Quilt Size: 57¼" x 73½"
Block Size: 11¾" x 11¾"
Number of Blocks: 12

Materials
- 2¾ yards white solid
- 6 (10") squares each light green, red, pink and dark green prints
- 1⅝ yards red dot
- ⅛ yard dark green print
- ⅝ yard light green dot
- 4⅞ yards backing
- 66" x 82" batting
- Thread
- Basic sewing tools and supplies

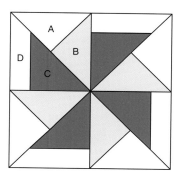

Pinwheel
11³/₄" x 11³/₄" Finished Block
Make 6

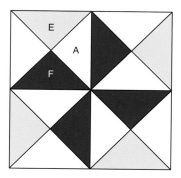

Electric Fan
11³/₄" x 11³/₄" Finished Block
Make 6

Project Notes

Read all instructions before beginning this project.

Stitch right sides together using a ¼" seam allowance unless otherwise specified.

Materials and cutting lists assume 40" of usable fabric width for yardage.

Arrows indicate directions to press seams.

WOF – width of fabric
HST – half-square triangle ◺
QST – quarter-square triangle ⊠

Cutting

From white solid cut:
- 18 (7⅛") A squares, then cut twice diagonally ⊠
- 24 (2¼" x 7") D rectangles
- 62 (2" x 12¼") J rectangles
- 80 (2") H squares

From each light green (10") square cut:
- 1 (7⅛") B square, then cut twice diagonally ⊠

From each red (10") square cut:
- 1 (7⅛") C square, then cut twice diagonally ⊠

From each pink (10") square cut:
- 1 (7⅛") E square, then cut twice diagonally ⊠

From each dark green (10") square cut:
- 1 (7⅛") F square, then cut twice diagonally ⊠

From red dot cut:
- 31 (2" x 12¼") K rectangles
- 80 (2") G squares
- 8 (2½" x WOF) binding strips

From dark green print cut:
- 20 (2") I squares

From light green dot cut:
- 7 (2½" x WOF) strips, stitch short ends to short ends, then subcut into:
    2 (2½" x 70") L and 2 (2½" x 57¾") M border strips

Completing the Blocks

1. Select four matching B and four matching C triangles for a Pinwheel block. Sew an A triangle to a B triangle to make an A-B unit (Figure 1). Make four A-B units.

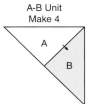

A-B Unit
Make 4

Figure 1

2. Sew a D rectangle to a C triangle, aligning the right angles as shown (Figure 2a). Open and press (Figure 2b). Trim the D rectangle even with the edge of the C triangle. This completes a C-D unit (Figure 2c). Make four C-D units.

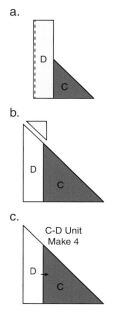

a.

b.

c.

C-D Unit
Make 4

Figure 2

3. Join an A-B unit and a C-D unit to make a Pinwheel quarter block (Figure 3). Make four quarter blocks.

Pinwheel Quarter Block
Make 4

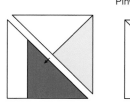

Figure 3

4. Arrange four quarter blocks into two rows of two as shown (Figure 4). Sew into rows and join the rows to complete a Pinwheel block. Repeat steps 1–4 to make six Pinwheel blocks.

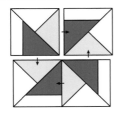

Make 6

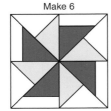

Figure 4

5. Select four matching E and four matching F triangles for an Electric Fan block. Sew an A triangle to an E triangle to make an A-E unit (Figure 5). Make four A-E units.

A-E Unit
Make 4

Figure 5

6. Sew an A triangle to an F triangle to make an A-F unit (Figure 6). Make four A-F units.

A-F Unit
Make 4

Figure 6

7. Join an A-E unit and an A-F unit to make an Electric Fan quarter block (Figure 7). Make four quarter blocks.

Electric Fan
Quarter Block
Make 4

Figure 7

8. Arrange four quarter blocks into two rows of two as shown (Figure 8). Sew into rows and join the rows to complete an Electric Fan block. Repeat steps 5–8 to make six Electric Fan blocks.

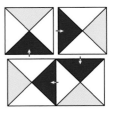

Make 6

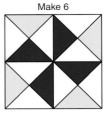

Figure 8

Completing the Sashing Units

1. Arrange four G squares, four H squares and one I square into three rows of three as shown (Figure 9). Sew into rows and join the rows to complete a nine-patch. Make 20 nine-patches.

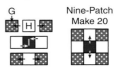

G   Nine-Patch
   H   Make 20

Figure 9

2. Sew J rectangles to the long sides of a K rectangle to make a sashing unit (Figure 10). Make 31 sashing units.

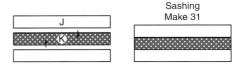

Sashing
Make 31

J
K

Figure 10

Completing the Quilt

1. Referring to the Assembly Diagram, lay out five sashing rows of four nine-patches and three sashing units each. Lay out four block rows of four sashing units and three blocks each, alternating Pinwheel and Electric Fan blocks as shown.

2. Sew the sashing rows and block rows and then join the rows, alternating, to complete the quilt center. Press.

3. Sew the L and M border strips to the quilt top in alphabetical order.

4. Layer, baste, quilt as desired and bind referring to Quilting Basics. The photographed quilt was hand-quilted in the ditch. ●

Sugar Lane
Assembly Diagram 57¼" x 73½"

Posy Patch

Use precut 10" squares of your favorite fabric collection to make this pretty patch of posies.

Designed & Quilted by Jen Daly of Jen Daly Quilts

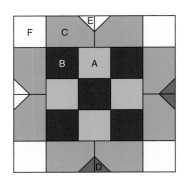

Corner
10" x 10" Finished Block
Make 4

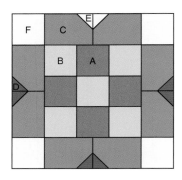

Side
10" x 10" Finished Block
Make 12

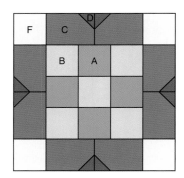

Middle
10" x 10" Finished Block
Make 9

Skill Level
Confident Beginner

Finished Sizes
Quilt Size: 68" x 68"
Block Size: 10" x 10"
Number of Blocks: 25

Materials
- 39 precut (10") squares assorted prints*
- 2 yards cream print*
- 1 yard blue floral*
- ¾ yard each green print and dark blue print*
- 4¼ yards backing*
- 76" x 76" batting
- Thread
- Basic sewing tools and supplies

Fabrics from the Mercantile collection by Lori Holt for Riley Blake Designs used to make sample. EQ8 was used to design this quilt.

Project Notes
Read all instructions before beginning this project.

Stitch right sides together using a ¼" seam allowance unless otherwise specified.

Materials and cutting lists assume 40" of usable fabric width for yardage.

Arrows indicate directions to press seams.

WOF – width of fabric
HST – half-square triangle ◻
QST – quarter-square triangle ⊠

"These pretty flower blocks started out with nine-patch centers for a cozy vintage feel, reminiscent of crocheted granny squares. Pieced sashing adds the illusion of leaves between the flowers." —Jen Daly

Cutting

From 1 print square cut:
- 16 (2½") I cornerstone squares

From each of 25 assorted print squares cut:
- 8 (2½" x 3½") C rectangles (200 total)
- 4 (2½") A squares (100 total)

From each of 13 assorted print squares cut:
- 10 (2½") B squares (130 total)

From length of cream print cut:
- 2 (2½" x 62½") K border strips
- 2 (2½" x 58½") J border strips
- 6 (4½" x 42") G strips
- 100 (2½") F squares
- 40 (1½") E squares

From blue floral cut:
- 7 (3½" x WOF) strips, stitch short ends to short ends, then subcut into:
  2 (3½" x 68½") M and 2 (3½" x 62½") L border strips

From green print cut:
- 3 (2½" x WOF) H strips
- 160 (1½") D squares

From dark blue print cut:
- 8 (2½" x WOF) binding strips

Completing the Nine-Patch Units

1. Arrange four matching A squares and five matching B squares alternating in three rows; sew into rows then sew the rows together to complete one nine-patch unit (Figure 1). Make 25. There will be five B squares leftover that will not be used.

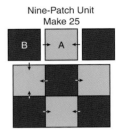

Nine-Patch Unit
Make 25

Figure 1

Completing the Blocks

Corner Blocks

1. To make one Corner block, choose one nine-patch unit, eight matching C rectangles and four each D squares, E squares and F squares.

2. Refer to Sew & Flip Corners to add a corner triangle on the upper right corner of one C rectangle using a D square to complete one left C-D unit. Repeat using an E square to make one left C-E unit (Figure 2). Make two of each.

Left C-D Unit
Make 2

Left C-E Unit
Make 2

Figure 2

SEW & FLIP CORNERS

Use this method to add triangle corners in a quilt block.

1. Draw a diagonal line from corner to corner on the wrong side of the specified square. Place the square, right sides together, on the indicated corner of the larger piece, making sure the line is oriented in the correct direction indicated by the pattern (Figure 1).

2. Sew on the drawn line. Trim ¼" away from sewn line (Figure 2).

3. Open and press to reveal the corner triangle (Figure 3).

Figure 1

Figure 2

Figure 3

4. If desired, square up the finished unit to the required unfinished size. ●

3. Repeat step 2, but position the corner triangles on the upper left corner of C to complete two each right C-D units and right C-E units (Figure 3).

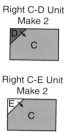

Right C-D Unit
Make 2

Right C-E Unit
Make 2

Figure 3

4. Sew a left C-D unit to the left of a right C-D unit to complete one C-D side unit. Then sew a left C-E unit to the left of a right C-E unit to complete one C-E side unit (Figure 4). Make two of each.

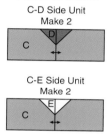

C-D Side Unit
Make 2

C-E Side Unit
Make 2

Figure 4

5. Noting fabric orientation, arrange the nine-patch unit, C-D side units, C-E side units and F squares into three rows; sew into rows, then sew the rows together to complete one Corner block (Figure 5).

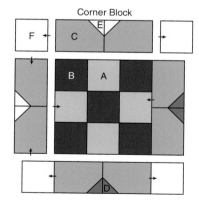

Corner Block

Figure 5

6. Repeat steps 1–5 to make four Corner blocks.

Side Blocks

1. To make one Side block, choose one nine-patch unit, eight matching C rectangles, six D squares, two E squares and four F squares.

2. Repeat steps 2–4 of Corner Blocks to make three C-D side units and one C-E side unit using the C rectangles, D squares and E squares.

3. Noting fabric orientation, arrange the nine-patch unit, C-D side units, C-E side unit and F squares into three rows; sew into rows, then sew the rows together to complete one Side block (Figure 6).

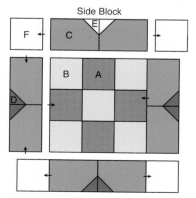

Side Block

Figure 6

4. Repeat steps 1–3 to make 12 Side blocks.

Middle Blocks

1. To make one Middle block, choose one nine-patch unit, eight matching C rectangles, eight D squares and four F squares.

2. Repeat steps 2–4 of Corner Blocks to make four C-D side units using the C rectangles and D squares.

3. Noting fabric orientation, arrange the nine-patch unit, C-D side units and F squares into three rows; sew into rows, then sew the rows together to complete one Middle block (Figure 7).

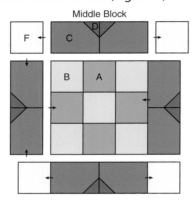

Middle Block

Figure 7

4. Repeat steps 1–3 to make nine Middle blocks.

Completing the Sashing Units

1. Sew one G strip to each long side of an H strip to make a strip set. Make three. Cut 40 (2½" x 10½") sashing units from the strip sets (Figure 8).

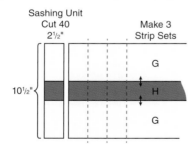

Sashing Unit
Cut 40
2½"

Make 3
Strip Sets

10½"

Figure 8

Completing the Quilt

1. Referring to the Assembly Diagram and noting block orientation, arrange the Corner blocks, Side blocks, Middle blocks, sashing units and I cornerstone squares in nine rows. Sew into rows, then sew the rows together to complete the quilt center.

2. Sew the J–M border strips onto the quilt center in alphabetical order to complete the quilt top.

3. Layer, baste, quilt as desired and bind referring to Quilting Basics. The photographed quilt was quilted with the Ginger Snap pantograph by Apricot Moon. ●

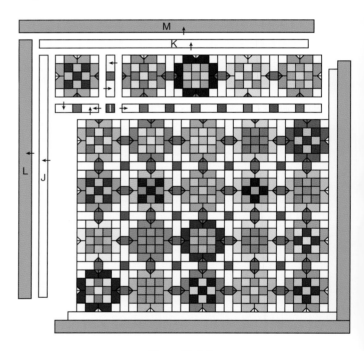

Posy Patch
Assembly Diagram 68" x 68"

Kindred Spirit

These log cabin blocks are perfect for a beginner
to learn the basics of quiltmaking.

Design by Wendy Sheppard
Quilted by Darlene Szabo of Sew Graceful Quilting

Skill Level
Confident Beginner

Finished Sizes
Runner Size: 44" x 16"
Block Size: 13" x 13"
Number of Blocks: 3

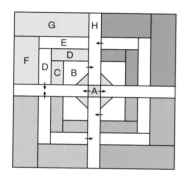

Maze
13" x 13" Finished Block
Make 3

Materials
- ½ yard background*
- 13 assorted 10" squares*
- ⅓ yard light print*
- ⅓ yard coral print*
- ¾ yard backing*
- 48" x 20" batting*
- Thread*
- Basic sewing tools and supplies

*Fabric from the Kindred collection by 1Canoe 2 for Moda Fabrics;
50 wt. Mako thread from Aurifil; Tuscany Silk batting from Hobbs Fibers
used to make sample. EQ8 was used to design this quilt.*

Project Notes

Read all instructions before beginning this project.

Stitch right sides together using a ¼" seam allowance unless otherwise specified.

Materials and cutting lists assume 40" of usable fabric width for yardage.

Arrows indicate directions to press seams.

WOF – width of fabric
HST – half-square triangle ◺
QST – quarter-square triangle ⊠

Cutting

From background cut:
- 12 (2½") B squares
- 2 (1½" x 13½") I rectangles
- 12 (1½" x 6½") H rectangles
- 12 (1½" x 4½") E rectangles
- 12 (1½" x 3½") D rectangles

From one 10" square cut:
- 15 (1½") A squares

From each remaining 10" square cut:
- 1 (2½" x 6½") G rectangle (12 total)
- 1 (2½" x 4½") F rectangle (12 total)
- 1 (1½" x 3½") D rectangle (12 total)
- 1 (1½" x 2½") C rectangle (12 total)

From light print cut:
- 4 (2" x WOF) strips, stitch short ends to short ends, then subcut into:
  - 2 (2" x 44½") K and
  - 2 (2" x 13½") J border strips

From coral print cut:
- 3 (2½" x WOF) binding strips

Completing the Blocks

1. Referring to Sew & Flip Corners on page 16, sew A squares to one corner of each B square to make 12 A-B units (Figure 1).

A-B Unit
Make 12

Figure 1

2. Sew matching print C, D, F and G rectangles and white D and E rectangles to the left and top sides of one A-B unit as shown to make 12 quarter block units (Figure 2).

Quarter Block Unit
Make 12

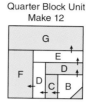

Figure 2

3. Refer to the Maze block diagram and arrange four quarter block units, four H rectangles and one A square in three rows, rotating quarter block units as shown. Sew together in rows; sew the rows together to complete one Maze block. Make three.

Here's a Tip

Make more blocks to turn this runner into a larger quilt.

Completing the Runner

1. Referring to the Assembly Diagram, arrange and sew the blocks and I rectangles together in one row.

2. Sew the J border strips to the short sides of the runner; sew the K border strips to the opposite long sides to complete the runner top.

3. Layer, baste, quilt as desired and bind referring to Quilting Basics. The photographed runner was quilted with a swirl design. ●

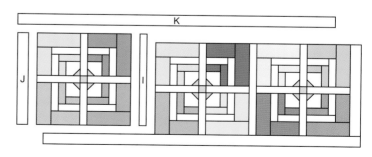

Kindred Spirit
Assembly Diagram 44" x 16"

Shanvi

Simple cuts and quick blocks make this a quilt that works up in no time.

Designed & Quilted by Preeti Harris of Sew Preeti Quilts

Skill Level
Confident Beginner

Finished Sizes
Quilt Size: 60" x 80"
Block Size: 10" x 10"
Number of Blocks: 35

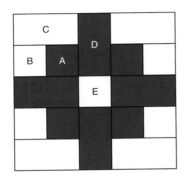

Block 1
10" x 10" Finished Block
Make 18

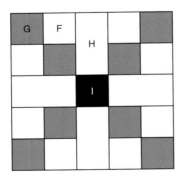

Block 2
10" x 10" Finished Block
Make 17

Materials
- 42 assorted precut 10" squares*
- ¼ yard black solid*
- ⅔ yard binding*
- 2⅞ yards white tonal*
- 5 yards backing*
- 68" x 88" batting
- Thread
- Basic sewing tools and supplies

Fabrics from the Fire and Ice by Claudia Pfeil and Neutral and Solid collections from Island Batik used to make sample.

Project Notes
Read all instructions before beginning this project.

Stitch right sides together using a ¼" seam allowance unless otherwise specified.

Arrows indicate directions to press seams.

Materials and cutting lists assume 40" of usable fabric width for yardage.

WOF – width of fabric
HST – half-square triangle ◻
QST – quarter-square triangle ⊠

Cutting

From each of 18 precut squares cut:
- 1 (5" x 10") rectangle, subcut into 4 (2½" x 4½") D rectangles
- 1 (5") A square
- 1 (5") square, subcut into 1 (4½") L square

From each of 17 precut squares cut:
- 2 (5") squares, subcut into 2 (4½") L squares
- 1 (5" x 10") rectangle, subcut into 2 (2½" x 10") G rectangles

From remaining 7 precut squares cut:
- 14 (4½") L squares

From black solid cut:
- 17 (2½") I squares

From binding fabric cut:
- 9 (2½" x WOF) binding strips

From white tonal cut:
- 34 (2½" x 10") F rectangles
- 36 (2½" x 9") C rectangles
- 36 (2½" x 5") B rectangles
- 68 (2½" x 4½") H rectangles
- 18 (2½") E squares
- 7 (1½" x WOF) strips, sew short ends to short ends, then subcut into:
    2 (1½" x 70½") J strips and 2 (1½" x 52½") K strips

Completing the Blocks

1. Working with A and D pieces from the same print, sew B rectangles lengthwise to opposite sides of one A square (Figure 1). Sew C rectangles to the top and bottom top make one A-B-C unit. Make one.

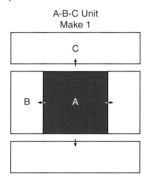

Figure 1

2. Cut into four equal corner units measuring 4½" square (Figure 2).

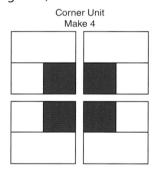

Figure 2

3. Lay out four corner units, one E square and four matching D rectangles into three rows of three (Figure 3). Sew into rows and join rows to make Block 1. Repeat steps 1–3 to make 18.

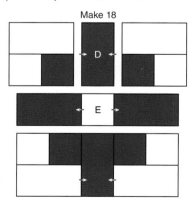

Figure 3

4. Sew one F rectangle to one G rectangle along long edges. Make two matching units. Crosscut each into four 2½" sections (Figure 4). Make a total of eight F-G units.

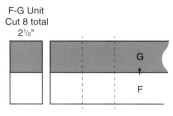

F-G Unit
Cut 8 total
2½"

Figure 4

5. Lay out two F-G units and sew together to make one four-patch unit (Figure 5). Make four.

Four-Patch Unit
Make 4

Figure 5

6. Lay out four four-patch units, four H rectangles and one I square into three rows of three (Figure 6). Sew into rows and join the rows to make Block 2. Repeat steps 4–6 to make 17.

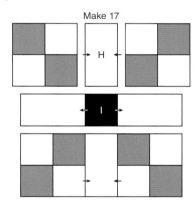

Make 17

Figure 6

Completing the Quilt

1. Lay out the blocks into seven rows of five blocks each, alternating blocks. Sew blocks into rows and join the rows to complete the quilt center.

2. Sew J strips to opposite sides of the quilt center. Sew K strips to the top and bottom.

3. Sew 18 L squares into a row to make a pieced side border. Make two. Sew to opposite sides of the quilt. Sew 15 L squares into a pieced top border. Repeat to make a pieced bottom border. Sew to the top and bottom.

4. Layer, baste, quilt as desired and bind referring to Quilting Basics. The photographed quilt was quilted with a wavy grid design. ●

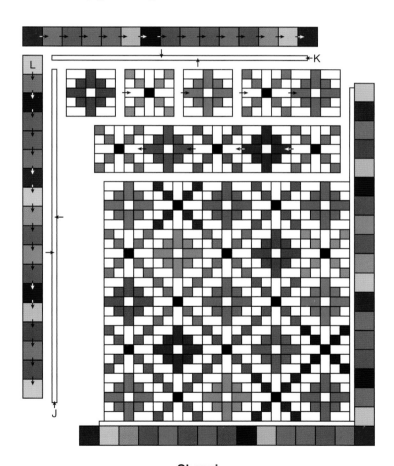

Shanvi
Assembly Diagram 60" x 80"

Heartfelt

A stack of precut 10" squares is perfect for a scrappy quilt where the fabrics play well together.

Design by Wendy Sheppard
Quilted by Darlene Szabo of Sew Graceful Quilting

Skill Level
Beginner

Finished Sizes
Quilt Size: 40" x 40"
Block Size: 8" x 8" and 4" x 8"
Number of Blocks: 22 and 6

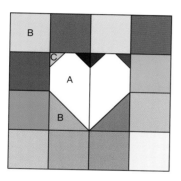

Heartfelt
8" x 8" Finished Block
Make 22

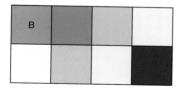

Half Block
4" x 8" Finished Block
Make 6

Materials
- 40 precut (10") squares assorted prints*
- ¾ yard white solid*
- ½ yard binding fabric*
- 2¾ yards backing*
- 48" x 48" batting*
- Thread*
- Basic sewing tools and supplies

*Fabrics from the 30's Playtime collection by Moda Fabrics; Aurifil 50 wt. Mako thread; Tuscany Silk batting from Hobbs used to make sample. EQ8 was used to design this quilt.

Project Notes
Read all instructions before beginning this project.

Stitch right sides together using a ¼" seam allowance unless otherwise specified.

Materials and cutting lists assume 40" of usable fabric width for yardage.

Arrows indicate directions to press seams.

WOF – width of fabric
HST – half-square triangle
QST – quarter-square triangle

Cutting

From assorted print squares cut:
- 356 total (2½") B squares
- 88 total (1¼") C squares

From white solid cut:
- 44 (2½" x 4½") A rectangles

From binding fabric cut:
- 5 (2½" x WOF) binding strips

Completing the Blocks

1. Refer to Sew & Flip Corners on page 16 to add corner triangles to the upper left and upper right corners of one A rectangle using two different C squares. Then add a corner triangle to the lower left corner using a different B square to complete one left A-B-C unit (Figure 1a). Make 22.

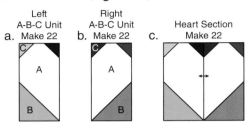

Figure 1

2. Repeat step 1 but position the B square on the lower right corner to complete 22 right A-B-C units (Figure 1b).

3. Sew one left A-B-C unit to the left of a right A-B-C unit to complete one heart section (Figure 1c). Make 22.

4. Arrange one heart section and 12 different B squares in three rows. First sew the B squares on the left of the heart section together, then sew the B squares on the right of the heart section together. Sew the units into rows and the rows together to complete one Heartfelt block (Figure 2). Make 22.

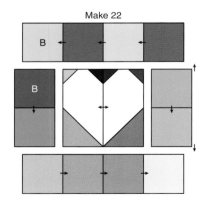

Make 22

Figure 2

5. Referring to the Half Block diagram, arrange eight different B squares in two rows; sew into rows, then sew the rows together to complete one Half Block. Press the top row left, bottom row right and the row seam down. Make six.

Completing the Quilt

1. Referring to the Assembly Diagram, arrange the Heartfelt blocks and Half blocks in five columns, making sure colors are evenly distributed. Sew the blocks into columns, then sew the columns together to complete the quilt top.

2. Stitch around the perimeter of the quilt top, close to the edge, to secure the seams.

3. Layer, baste, quilt as desired and bind referring to Quilting Basics. The photographed quilt was quilted with an allover arc design. ●

Heartfelt
Assembly Diagram 40" x 40"

Holiday Cheer

Capture the essence of holiday nostalgia with this charming red and green table runner.

Designed & Quilted by Jen Shaffer

Skill Level
Confident Beginner

Finished Sizes
Quilt Size: 20" x 68"
Block Size: 16" x 16"
Number of Blocks: 4

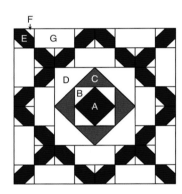

Holiday Cheer Red
16" x 16" Finished Block
Make 2

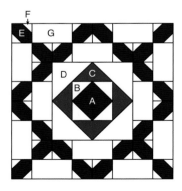

Holiday Cheer Green
16" x 16" Finished Block
Make 2

Materials
- 1½ yards cream*
- ½ yard dark green*
- 1 fat quarter light green*
- ⅞ yards dark red*
- 1 fat quarter light red*
- 1½ yards backing*
- 24" x 72" batting
- Thread
- Basic sewing tools and supplies

*Fabric from the Cotton Shot collection from Benartex used to make sample.

Project Notes
Read all instructions before beginning this project.

Stitch right sides together using a ¼" seam allowance unless otherwise specified.

Materials and cutting lists assume 40" of usable fabric width for yardage and 20" for fat quarters.

Arrows indicate directions to press seams.

WOF – width of fabric
HST – half-square triangle ◳
QST – quarter-square triangle ◲

Cutting

From cream cut:
- 8 (4⅞") D squares, cut diagonally once to make 16 HSTs ◳
- 8 (2⅞") B squares, cut diagonally once to make 16 HSTs ◳
- 48 (2½" x 4½") G rectangles
- 5 (2½" x WOF) strips, stitch short ends to short ends, then subcut into:
    2 (2½" x 64½") H and 2 (2½" x 20½") I border strips
- 192 (1½") F squares

Inspiration

"My memories of Christmas at my grandparents' home include a stair railing with garland and stockings in colorful greens and reds." —Jen Shaffer

From dark green cut:

- 2 (3⅜") A squares
- 48 (2½") E squares

From light green cut:

- 4 (3⅝") C squares, cut diagonally once to make 8 HSTs ◰

From dark red cut:

- 2 (3⅜") A squares
- 5 (2½" x WOF) binding strips
- 48 (2½") E squares

From light red cut:

- 4 (3⅝") C squares, cut diagonally once to make 8 HSTs ◰

Here's a Tip

Check orientation of units at each step to ensure accuracy.

Completing the Units

1. Sew cream B triangles to opposite sides of one dark green A square (Figure 1); press. Sew cream B triangles to remaining sides of A square to make a green square-in-a-square unit. Repeat to make two green units and two red units.

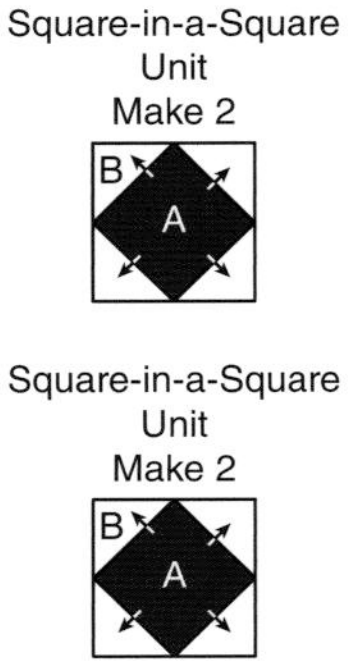

Square-in-a-Square
Unit
Make 2

Square-in-a-Square
Unit
Make 2

Figure 1

2. In a similar manner, sew a light green C triangle to each side of a green square-in-a-square unit as shown (Figure 2). Repeat to add cream D triangles to complete green unit A. Make two green and two red unit A.

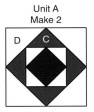

Unit A
Make 2

Unit A
Make 2

Figure 2

3. Refer to Sew & Flip Corners on page 16 and use the dark green E squares and cream F squares to make 48 green unit B (Figure 3). Repeat to make 48 red unit B.

Unit B
Make 48

Unit B
Make 48

Figure 3

4. Sew together two matching unit B to make a unit C. Make 16 green and 16 red unit C (Figure 4).

Unit C
Make 16

Unit C
Make 16

Figure 4

5. Sew together one cream G rectangle and two matching unit B to make unit D (Figure 5). Make four green and four red unit D.

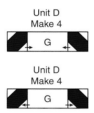

Unit D
Make 4

Unit D
Make 4

Figure 5

6. Sew together one cream G rectangle and two matching unit C as shown to make unit E (Figure 6). Make four green and four red unit E.

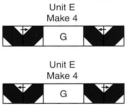

Unit E
Make 4

Unit E
Make 4

Figure 6

7. Sew together one unit C and two cream G rectangles as shown to make unit F (Figure 7). Make eight green and eight red unit F.

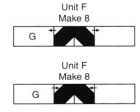

Unit F
Make 8

Unit F
Make 8

Figure 7

8. Sew together one matching unit F and two matching unit B to make unit G (Figure 8). Make four green and four red unit G.

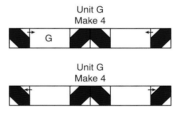

Unit G
Make 4

Unit G
Make 4

Figure 8

Completing the Blocks

1. Sew red unit D to opposite sides of red unit A as shown (Figure 9).

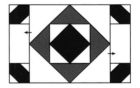

Figure 9

2. Sew red unit E to top and bottom (Figure 10).

Figure 10

3. Sew two red unit F to opposite sides as shown (Figure 11).

Figure 11

4. Sew two red unit G to top and bottom as shown to complete Holiday Cheer Red block (Figure 12). Make two. Repeat to complete two Holiday Cheer Green blocks.

Red Block
Make 2

Green Block
Make 2

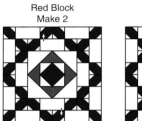

Figure 12

Completing the Runner

1. Referring to Assembly Diagram, lay out blocks as shown and sew together.

2. Sew the H and I border strips to the quilt top in alphabetical order.

3. Layer, baste, quilt as desired and bind referring to Quilting Basics. The photographed quilt was quilted with an overall meander design. ●

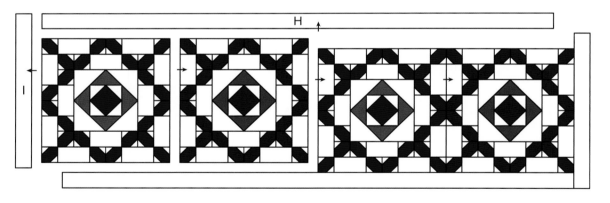

Holiday Cheer
Assembly Diagram 20" x 68"

Riverscape View

Grab a package of 10" precut squares and some background fabric and you'll have a great gift or decor-matching quilt in no time!

Designed & Quilted by Rachelle Craig

Skill Level
Confident Beginner

Finished Sizes
Quilt Size: 40" x 48"
Block Size: 8" x 8"
Number of Blocks: 30

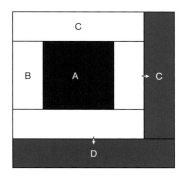

Courthouse Steps Variation
8" x 8" Finished Block
Make 30

Materials
- 23 assorted 10" squares*
- 1⅛ yards white*
- ½ yard bright blue*
- 2½ yards backing*
- 44" x 52" batting*
- Thread
- Basic sewing tools and supplies

*Fabric from the Flora and Fauna: Midnight by Amanda Murphy and Color Weave by Contempo Studios collections for Benartex; Tuscany Wool/Cotton Blend Batting by Hobbs Bonded Fibers used to make sample.

Project Notes
Read all instructions before beginning this project.

Stitch right sides together using a ¼" seam allowance unless otherwise specified.

Materials and cutting lists assume 40" of usable fabric width for yardage.

Arrows indicate directions to press seams.

WOF – width of fabric
HST – half-square triangle ◻
QST – quarter-square triangle ⊠

Cutting

From eight 10" squares cut:
- 30 (4") A squares

From each remaining 10" square cut:
- 2 (2" x 8½") D rectangles (30 total)
- 2 (2" x 7") C rectangles (30 total)

From white cut:
- 60 (2" x 7") C rectangles
- 60 (2" x 4") B rectangles

From bright blue cut:
- 5 (2½" x WOF) binding strips

Completing the Blocks
1. Sew a B rectangle on opposite sides of an A square (Figure 1). Make 30.

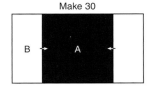

Figure 1

Inspiration

"I needed a simple child-size quilt for a gift for a close friend's daughter. I had some various bright-colored 10" precut squares left over from a couple of previous projects, so I put them all together and Riverscape View was created!" —Rachelle Craig

2. Sew a white C rectangle on the top and bottom of step 1 units (Figure 2). Make 30.

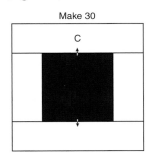

Make 30

Figure 2

3. Referring to the Courthouse Steps Variation block diagram, sew matching print C and D rectangles to one step 2 unit to complete one Courthouse Steps Variation block. Make 30.

Completing the Quilt

1. Referring to the Assembly Diagram, arrange the blocks randomly in six rows of five blocks.

2. Sew the blocks together in rows; join the rows to complete the quilt top.

3. Layer, baste, quilt as desired and bind referring to Quilting Basics. The photographed quilt was quilted using a serpentine stitch in a grid pattern. ●

Here Are Tips

Press seams toward the outside as you go; it makes adding the next piece easier.

If you have a full (40) piece package of precut squares, you can also make a scrappy binding. Cut 21½" x 10" strips and piece them together to make at least 190" of binding.

When using a scrappy binding, make the first and last pieces of the binding the same color; this helps hide the final binding join.

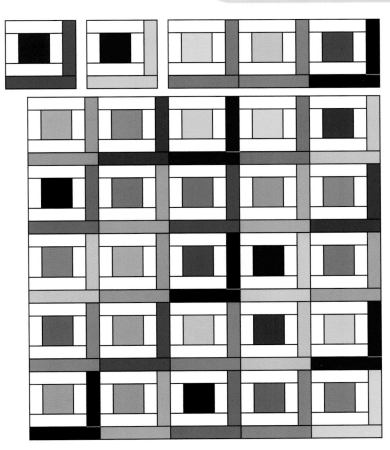

Riverscape View
Assembly Diagram 40" x 48"

Garden Sun

Enjoy the vibrant energy and warmth of summer with this colorful table runner.

Designed & Quilted by Gina Gempesaw

Skill Level
Confident Beginner

Finished Sizes
Table Runner Size: 40" x 16"
Block Size: 12" x 12"
Number of Blocks: 3

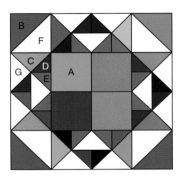

Garden Sun
12" x 12" Finished Block
Make 3

Materials
- 1 (5") square each 24 assorted medium value prints
- 1 (3") square each 24 assorted dark value prints
- ⅝ yard white tonal
- ½ yard gray print
- 1 yard backing
- 26" x 50" batting
- Thread
- Basic sewing tools and supplies

Project Notes
Read all instructions before beginning this project.

Stitch right sides together using a ¼" seam allowance unless otherwise specified.

Materials and cutting lists assume 41" of usable fabric width for yardage.

Arrows indicate directions to press seams.

WOF – width of fabric
HST – half-square triangle ◱
QST – quarter-square triangle ⊠

Cutting

From assorted medium value prints cut:
- 6 (4¼") C squares, then cut twice diagonally ⊠
- 6 (3⅞") B squares, then cut once diagonally ◱
- 12 (3½") A squares

From assorted dark value prints cut:
- 24 (2⅜") D squares, then cut once diagonally ◱

From white tonal cut:
- 9 (4¼") G squares, then cut twice diagonally ⊠
- 6 (3⅞") F squares, then cut once diagonally ◱
- 2 (2½" x 12½") H border strips
- 2 (2½" x 40½") I border strips

From gray print cut:
- 12 (2⅜") E squares, then cut once diagonally ◱
- 3 (2½" x WOF) binding strips

Completing the Garden Sun Blocks

1. Arrange four A squares in two rows and sew together to complete a four-patch unit (Figure 1). Make three.

Four-Patch Unit
Make 3

Figure 1

2. Sew one each B and F triangle together to complete a B-F unit (Figure 2). Make 12.

B-F Unit
Make 12

Figure 2

3. Sew two different D triangles together to complete a D-D unit (Figure 3). Make 12.

D-D Unit
Make 12

Figure 3

4. Sew a G triangle onto each side of one D-D unit to complete a G-D-D unit (Figure 4). Make 12.

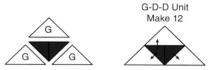

G-D-D Unit
Make 12

Figure 4

5. Arrange one each C, D and E triangle into a triangle shape with D placed in the middle and sew together to complete a left C-D-E unit (Figure 5a). Make 12.

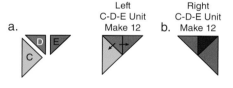

a.   Left C-D-E Unit Make 12   b.   Right C-D-E Unit Make 12

Figure 5

6. Noting fabric orientation, repeat step 5 using the remaining C, D and E triangles to complete 12 right C-D-E units (Figure 5b).

7. Sew a left C-D-E unit to the left side of a G-D-D unit and a right C-D-E unit to the right to complete a side center section (Figure 6). Make 12.

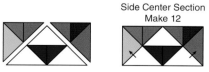

Side Center Section
Make 12

Figure 6

8. Arrange one four-patch unit and four each B-F units and side center sections into three rows (Figure 7). Sew into rows and then sew the rows together to complete one Garden Sun block. Make three.

Make 3

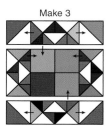

Figure 7

Completing the Runner

1. Referring to the Assembly Diagram, sew the blocks together in a row to complete the table runner center.

2. Sew H border strips to the short sides of the center and I border strips to the long sides to complete the table runner top.

3. Refer to Quilting Basics to layer and baste the table runner. Quilt as desired.

4. Prepare binding strips referring to Quilting Basics and bind the table runner.

5. The photographed table runner was quilted with a sunburst design. ●

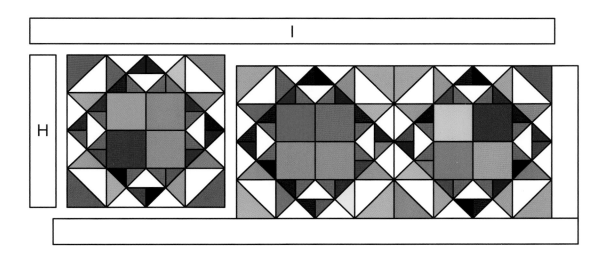

Garden Sun
Assembly Diagram 40" x 16"

Log Cabin Jam

Lose yourself in your favorite fat quarter bundle while making a sparkling rainbow of log cabin blocks. Three different sizes of simple blocks add interest and challenge to the project.

Designed & Quilted by Jennifer Strauser of Dizzy Quilter

Skill Level
Confident Beginner

Finished Sizes
Quilt Size: 48" x 60"
Block Sizes: 12" x 12", 6" x 6" and 3" x 3"
Number of Blocks: 10, 30 and 40

Materials
- 25 fat quarters (5 color groups in 5 step gradations)
- ⅝ yard binding
- 4 yards backing fabric
- 57" x 69" batting
- Thread
- Basic sewing tools and supplies

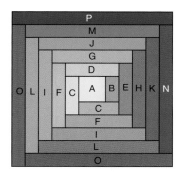

Block 1
12" x 12" Finished Block
Make 10

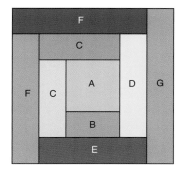

Block 2
6" x 6" Finished Block
Make 20

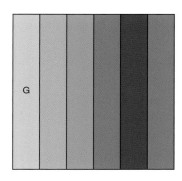

Block 3
6" x 6" Finished Block
Make 5

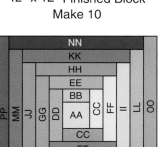

Block 4
6" x 6" Finished Block
Make 5

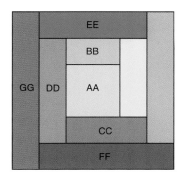

Block 5
3" x 3" Finished Block
Make 30

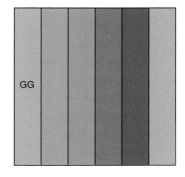

Block 6
3" x 3" Finished Block
Make 10

Project Notes

Read all instructions before beginning this project.

Stitch right sides together using a ¼" seam allowance unless otherwise specified.

Materials and cutting lists assume 40" of usable fabric width for yardage and 20" for fat quarters.

Press seams open throughout.

WOF – width of fabric
HST – half-square triangle
QST – quarter-square triangle

Cutting

Note: *Separate your fabrics into five groups of five based on value, from Group 1 (lightest value) through Group 5 (darkest value). Stack fabrics by group and cut through all five fabrics in each group at one time to make the indicated total number of pieces.*

From Group 1 cut a total of:

- 30 (2½") A squares
- 5 (1½" x 6½") G rectangles
- 10 (1½" x 4½") D rectangles
- 20 (1½" x 3½") C rectangles
- 10 (1½" x 2½") B rectangles
- 35 (1½") AA squares
- 10 (1" x 3½") GG rectangles
- 5 (1" x 2½") DD rectangles
- 10 (1" x 2") CC rectangles
- 5 (1" x 1½") BB rectangles

From Group 2 cut a total of:

- 15 (1½" x 6½") G rectangles
- 20 (1½" x 5½") F rectangles
- 10 (1½" x 4½") E rectangles
- 15 (1" x 3½") GG rectangles
- 10 (1" x 3") FF rectangles

From Group 3 cut a total of:

- 10 (1½" x 8½") J rectangles
- 20 (1½" x 7½") I rectangles
- 10 (1½" x 6½") H rectangles
- 5 (1½" x 6½") G rectangles
- 20 (1½" x 4½") D rectangles
- 40 (1½" x 3½") C rectangles
- 20 (1½" x 2½") B rectangles
- 5 (1" x 4½") JJ rectangles
- 10 (1" x 4") II rectangles
- 5 (1" x 3½") HH rectangles
- 10 (1" x 3½") GG rectangles
- 30 (1" x 2½") DD rectangles
- 60 (1" x 2") CC rectangles
- 30 (1" x 1½") BB rectangles

From Group 4 cut a total of:

- 10 (1½" x 10½") M rectangles
- 20 (1½" x 9½") L rectangles
- 10 (1½" x 8½") K rectangles
- 10 (1½" x 6½") G rectangles
- 40 (1½" x 5½") F rectangles
- 20 (1½" x 4½") E rectangles
- 10 (1" x 5½") LL rectangles
- 5 (1" x 4½") KK rectangles
- 15 (1" x 3½") GG rectangles
- 60 (1" x 3") FF rectangles
- 35 (1" x 2½") EE rectangles

From Group 5 cut a total of:

- 10 (1½" x 12½") P rectangles
- 20 (1½" x 11½") O rectangles
- 10 (1½" x 10½") N rectangles
- 25 (1½" x 6½") G rectangles
- 5 (1" x 6½") PP rectangles
- 10 (1" x 6") OO rectangles
- 5 (1" x 5½") MM rectangles
- 5 (1" x 5½") NN rectangles
- 45 (1" x 3½") GG rectangles

From binding fabric cut:

- 6 (2½" x WOF) binding strips

Completing the Blocks

1. Sew one B rectangle to the right side of one A square (Figure 1). Sew one C rectangle to the bottom.

Figure 1

2. Sew one C rectangle to the left side of the unit from step 1 (Figure 2). Sew one D rectangle to the top.

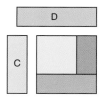

Figure 2

3. In the same way, continue adding rectangles in a clockwise manner to make one of Block 1, ending with one P rectangle and measuring 12½" square unfinished (Figure 3). Make 10, varying color placement and always working from lighter values to darker values.

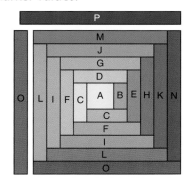

Figure 3

4. In the same way, starting with one A square and ending with one G rectangle, make 20 of Block 2, measuring 6½" square unfinished.

5. Starting with one AA square, add BB, CC and DD rectangles around the square clockwise (Figure 4). In the same way, refer to the Block 4 diagram and continue adding rectangles in alphabetical order, ending with one PP rectangle and measuring 6½" square unfinished. Make five of Block 4.

Figure 4

6. In the same way, starting with one AA square and ending with one GG rectangle, make 30 of Block 5, measuring 3½" square unfinished.

7. Lay out six G rectangles, ranging from light to dark (Figure 5). Use one rectangle from each group, plus one extra from group 4. Sew the six G rectangles together to make one Block 3, measuring 6½" square unfinished. Make five.

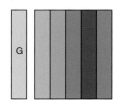

Figure 5

8. In the same way, lay out six GG rectangles from light to dark to make one Block 6, measuring 3½" square unfinished. Make 10.

Completing the Quilt

1. Referring to the Assembly Diagram, lay out combinations of Blocks 2–6 into block units measuring 12½" square. Join combinations of four of Block 5 and 6 into two rows of two, and then join the rows. Combine these units with 6½" square blocks to make block units. Make a total of 10 large block units.

2. Lay out the 10 large block units and 10 of Block 1 into five rows of four each. Sew into rows and join the rows to complete the quilt top.

3. Layer, quilt as desired and bind referring to Quilting Basics. The photographed quilt was quilted with an allover starry design. ●

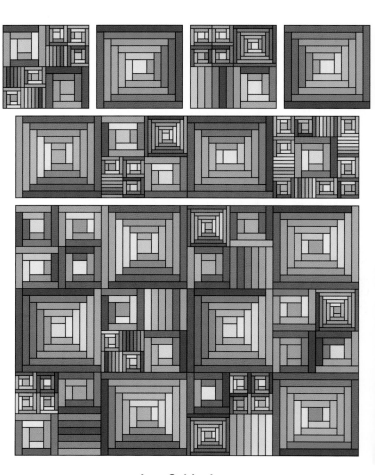

Log Cabin Jam
Assembly Diagram 48" x 60"

Quilting Basics

The following is a reference guide. For more information, consult a comprehensive quilting book.

Quilt Backing & Batting

Cut your backing and batting 8" larger than the finished quilt-top size and 4" larger for quilts smaller than 50" square. *Note: Check with longarm quilter about their requirements, if applicable. For baby quilts not going to a longarm quilter 4"–6" overall may be sufficient.* If preparing the backing from standard-width fabrics, remove the selvages and sew two or three lengths together; press seams open. If using 108"-wide fabric, trim to size on the straight grain of the fabric. Prepare batting the same size as your backing.

Quilting

1. Press quilt top on both sides and trim all loose threads. ***Note:** If you are sending your quilt to a longarm quilter, contact them for specifics about preparing your quilt for quilting.*
2. Mark quilting design on quilt top. Make a quilt sandwich by layering the backing right side down, batting and quilt top centered right side up on flat surface and smooth out. Baste layers together using pins, thread basting or spray basting to hold. ***Note:** Tape or pin backing to surface to hold taut while layering and avoid puckers.*
3. Quilt as desired by hand or machine. Remove pins or basting as you quilt.
4. Trim batting and backing edges even with raw edges of quilt top.

Binding the Quilt

1. Join binding strips on short ends with diagonal seams to make one long strip; trim seams to ¼" and press seams open (Figure 1).

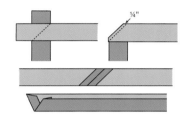

Figure 1

2. Fold ½" of one short end to wrong side and press. Fold the binding strip in half with wrong sides together along length, again referring to Figure 1; press.
3. Starting about 3" from the folded short end, sew binding to quilt top edges, matching raw edges and using a ¼" seam. Stop stitching ¼" from corner and backstitch (Figure 2).

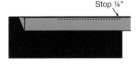

Figure 2

4. Fold binding up at a 45-degree angle to seam and then down even with quilt edges, forming a pleat at corner (Figure 3).

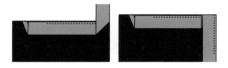

Figure 3

5. Resume stitching from corner edge as shown in Figure 3, down quilt side, backstitching ¼" from next corner. Repeat, mitering all corners, stitching to within 3" of starting point.
6. Trim binding, leaving enough length to tuck inside starting end and complete stitching (Figure 4).

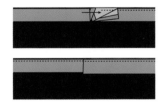

Figure 4

7. If stitching binding by hand, machine-sew binding to the front of the quilt and fold to the back before stitching. If stitching by machine, machine-sew binding to back of the quilt and fold to the front before stitching.

Special Thanks

Please join us in thanking the talented designers
whose work is featured in this collection.

Lyn Brown
New Growth, 3

Rachelle Craig
Riverscape View, 35

Jen Daly
Posy Patch, 14

Gina Gempesaw
Garden Sun, 39

Preeti Harris
Shanvi, 22

Amy Krasnansky
March of Diamonds, 7

Jill Metzger
Sugar Lane, 9

Jen Shaffer
Holiday Cheer, 30

Wendy Sheppard
Kindred Spirit, 19
Heartfelt, 27

Jennifer Strauser
Log Cabin Jam, 43

Supplies

We would like to thank the following manufacturers who provided
materials to our designers to make sample projects for this book.

New Growth, page 3: Fabric from Hoffman California-International Fabrics used to make sample.

Posy Patch, page 14: Fabrics from the Mercantile collection by Lori Holt for Riley Blake Designs used to make sample. EQ8 was used to design this quilt.

Kindred Spirit, page 19: Fabric from the Kindred collection by 1Canoe 2 for Moda Fabrics; 50 wt. Mako thread from Aurifil; Tuscany Silk batting from Hobbs Fibers used to make sample. EQ8 was used to design this quilt.

Shanvi, page 22: Fabrics from the Fire and Ice by Claudia Pfeil and Neutral and Solid collections from Island Batik to make sample.

Heartfelt, page 27: Fabrics from the 30's Playtime collection by Moda Fabrics; Aurifil Mako 50 wt. thread; Tuscany Silk batting from Hobbs used to make sample. EQ8 was used to design this quilt.

Holiday Cheer, page 30: Fabric from the Cotton Shot collection from Benartex used to make sample.

Riverscape View, page 35: Fabric from the Flora and Fauna: Midnight by Amanda Murphy and Color Weave by Contempo Studios collections for Benartex; Tuscany Wool/Cotton Blend Batting by Hobbs Bonded Fibers used to make sample.

 Published by Annie's, 306 East Parr Road, Berne, IN 46711. Printed in USA. Copyright © 2024 Annie's. All rights reserved. This publication may not be reproduced in part or in whole without written permission from the publisher.

RETAIL STORES: If you would like to carry this publication or any other Annie's publications, visit AnniesWSL.com.

Every effort has been made to ensure that the instructions in this publication are complete and accurate. We cannot, however, take responsibility for human error, typographical mistakes or variations in individual work. Please visit AnniesCustomerService.com to check for pattern updates.

ISBN: 979-8-89253-348-5

1 2 3 4 5 6 7 8 9